THE MARKETING GURU

Capitalism for Dummies and How to Get Yours

"If someone can do it better, let them. If you can do it better, it's God's way of saying it's your job"-Anonymous

A Publication of Philanthropic Cultural Expressions, Inc.

By Carrington B. Davis, BA Econ, MBA, MPA

© Washington, DC 2012

Table of Contents

In this fast paced, high technology world that we live in, it's difficult to get a handle on some of the disciplines that one needs to be successful. This is especially true in the field of business, where the push for entrepreneurialism is the current trend. To survive, you need to have a spiritual fervor and a proper understanding of what works, why and how.

"Business", as President Calvin Coolidge once put it, "is the business of America". Entrepreneurialism is, therefore, not a new phenomenon, but a fabric of our economy and culture. After all, we live in a "free enterprise system" and people with a desire to make a go at it need to understand what the system is all about. They need the skills and practices of business, that which can be obtained from a textbook, to master the science of business. And, they need the discipline of <u>thinking</u> and <u>feeling</u> the way business is done, as well. They need to be able to talk about business as if it were an Art, which it is.

This book is designed to meet the growing need for a method of understanding marketing as an essential function of business, and how to perform that function. In today's world, businesses, nonprofit organizations, and governments are all required to use marketing techniques in competition for the interest and involvement of the buying public. Everything from cars, to the corporate images, to the Councilman's campaign can be marketed to the public, and is. The transportation industry and the mass-media complex, both owe their growth and power to a link with the marketing system of the nation. Conversely, the growth and development of businesses, nonprofits, and the ideas and policies of governments are based on the expansion and refinement of the marketing system. An understanding of the marketing system, how it works, and the methods and means of benefiting from it, whether you operate a corner grocery store, a neighborhood museum, or sell cookies on weekends, makes you an effective entrepreneur.

As an effective entrepreneur, you must appreciate both the conceptual aspects of marketing, or how it all fits together; and the practical aspects of marketing, or how to make it fit your needs. In this light, this book is designed to guide the reader through the concepts of marketing, the "feeling" for it, and the process of thinking and planning the progress of your organization from a marketing point-of-view. The emphasis is placed on understanding how to find your place, or your organization's place, in the whirlwind of competition and socio-technological change that surrounds the marketplace. It's like a trip to the top of a mountain, from which you can see the entire marketing system. And from that point of view, you are able to determine how to plan your marketing program to reach realistic success. From that point of view, you can see how to measure, manage and implement your concepts, seize coming opportunities, and properly utilize your resources. It's your business, your marketplace and your decisions. In this book, it's my job to provide the road map. Drive with care and keep on believing.

Chapter 1- The Entrepreneurial Economy and the New Tools

New Age, new space, new day, new race
New people, new pace, be friends on MySpace
Get schooled, get ruled, get jeweled, get fooled
Get made, get laid, get frayed, get paid
New world, new day, each and everyone can play

I met a man who I call the Marketing Guru while I was smoking a cigar and reading the paper at the /Washington Harbor complex in Georgetown in Washington, DC. The Washington Harbor is a restaurant and entertainment development with a tall flag tower in the middle of a broad circular fountain with foliage arranged in around and inside the fountain I would sit on the benches attached to the tree boxes on the veranda above the fountain that was separated by a brick staircase leading down to the fountain and out to the Potomac River.

I would go to the Washington Harbor, smoke a cigar, drink a cup of coffee and relax or read a paper. The boardwalk along the river provides a promenade of people, dogs, bikes and strollers that float gently throughout the day. From my vantage on the veranda, on a perfect day, you can see a picture perfect view of the bars on each side of the stairway leading to the Potomac River, with its boats, crews and panoramic view of the Kennedy Center and the tree-filled Roosevelt Island on the Virginia side.

I would sit and ponder whatever I was pondering at the time. On this day, I was pondering the writing of this book. On a fine summer afternoon, I was pondering over a copy of the Financial Times of London when I met this man who walked by and said, "That's a nice cigar. What kind is it? I replied, "Arturo Fuentes 858".

"Nice!" He said as he passed.

About a week passed, after more pondering about saying some things I thought would clarify the understanding of the application and purpose of the

Principles of Marketing, I ran into him at Georgetown Tobacco as I sat and talked with the wise and intellectual patronage and officialdoms. He came in and joined in the seating section where cigar smokers, those that remain, solve the problems of the world and give needed advice to gamblers and risk-takers who deal in Fantasy Sports and Washington politics.

I didn't see him until a week before I wrote this book when I ran into him at a coffee shop on K Street. He was inline ahead of me and turned around, looked at me and said "Are you following me"? I laughed and we struck up a conversation and sat down.

He was a man in his 80's, I discovered in our talk and carried a countenance of sparse gray hair that swirled about his crown as if it were a cotton candy cap without a bill. He was short, about 5 feet five inches tall. His eyes were a deep dark brown and they contained a hint of intensity within. He looked like a 15-year old when he smiled. He sort of became my guru for telling me what it is I needed to understand about economics and the art and artistry of the Marketing discipline.

You might say he was an Entrepreneur, new age pioneer and explorer. We sat and this is what I got out of our first real sit-down. I told him I was thinking about writing a book on Marketing to help students get more of a sense of it, and he began his guidance to me with a look, and a quip. He said, "Always remember this. As the Bible says, along with other religious texts in many places on this planet, *seek and ye shall find*. Remember that", he added. He sipped a bit of his coffee and continued.

If you are trying to make it on your own in business in America, you need to understand Capitalism. A lot of people talk about capitalism, but very few people know anything about it. Capitalism evolved from economic systems created around monarchy and Royal ownership, and the accompanying grants, charters and rights given by the Crown. This was a system where the Crown gives right to land, trade, commerce or property. All of this, like modern banking, was developed during the centuries following the discovery of America and the economic systems needed to exploit the colonies. That was the system that evolves into Capitalism.

One explanation of Capitalism is that it shows us how rational self-interest in a free-market economy leads to economic well-being. A dictionary definition of Capitalism would include private property rights, free enterprise, and the elements of land, labor, capital and entrepreneurship. Adam Smith believed that the wealth of Nations was dependent upon the productivity of labor and he argued about the availability of land at a time when the French and the English and the Spanish were struggling for control of vast lands that they could not even survey. The wealth of

Nations was dependent upon many things, but labor was the key element in developing the New World. After all, land wasn't a problem, nor was capital or willing entrepreneurs. Labor can provide a competitive advantage. So keep that in mind as we learn more about how the economy works. That's called macroeconomics. How your business works is called microeconomics.

Capitalism also talks about an invisible hand. The concept is somewhat like a God that oversees the natural flow of things. That God, that invisible hand, is the free will in the marketplace of the ideas of anybody and everybody that can join in. There'll some discussions about government and the role of government that comes out of Adam Smith, but this is not the time to talk about that. That comes under marketing intelligence later on.

Adam Smith talked about the market as a competitive place. A place where individuals would be paid more for work that required more learning or that was more difficult. He also talked about the marketplace as a competitive arena. A marketplace where resources are, allowing for differences in risk, allocated to the highest and best use. It's like a bidding system. And remember, all this happened around 1776.

If you remember the world of 1776, and the America of 1776, it will make sense that Adam Smith proposed competitive advantage for nations that had one or more such advantages in world trade.

Remember also that this was a time of global abolitionism. The Slave Trade was abolished in the British Empire in 1807. The British Empire Abolish slavery throughout in 1834, but all this began with a judgment in the Somerset Case that emancipated a slave in 1772. So it was a different world then. But that is the system, the macroeconomic system, in which we operate a business, as a microeconomic legal entity. And all of this is summed up in the entrepreneur. Entrepreneur, a word derived from the French that generally means a person who initiates a business or enterprise and takes on a measurable degree of risk. Entrepreneurs organize and manage land, labor and capital.

To Adam Smith, the Wealth of Nations came from the productive portion of the population. The productive portion of the population is led by enterprising people who have the blessings of the Crown to pursue the best interest of the Crown. That's the way it was in 1776. It was like Columbus Discovering America. He did it for Queen Isabella or it was no go. Yet, in America there was the independence of labor, even though there was the enslavement of labor as part of the wealth development of America is concerned. I'm glad we are over that.

What we need to take away from this is this. Adam Smith recognized that the individual was a key an important factor in the development of all nations, European monarchies and the emerging American colonies, in a world where the individual was becoming en franchised. Systems of labor have evolved from being controlled by the Crown, to oversight of craft guilds, to overseers of the apprentice system, to labor unions to professional societies and business people who are free to invest and take risks for themselves, by themselves or together.

In 1776, the world was emerging from a monarchy into a world ruled by merchants and bankers. With the discovery of the New World, and the institutions created by the Colonists, the "free enterprise system", the "free market" will as a democratic political system that encompasses individual freedom civil rights, rights to property and a legal system to resolve disputes secures the blessings of peace for us and our posterity as a quasi-laissez faire economy. And then, there was all that land.

The significant thing about Adam Smith is that he wrote that a cooperative, individually centered society, operating in self interests in a free exchange, seeking the highest and best use would be more valuable than a society ruled by kings who distributed wealth according to their dictate. That sounds a lot like a democratic system to me, a democratic economy. He also wrote that people can be both self-interested and philanthropic as well. Cooperation and compassion are an integral part of his philosophy of how we deal with each other economically in this Post-King and Queen world.

The system is supposed to be self-sustaining and self-supporting with the Invisible Hand guiding us all to prosperity and peace. That's the dream of it all.

From all this, we now understand that America's entrepreneurs succeed through collaboration and cooperation, not competition. There's plenty for everybody. So be sure you join every trade association, professional society, merchant group, charitable cause, commercial district, business group, industry coalition and political interest group that you can.

Capitalism is cooperation. Some take the low road and see it as "every man for himself" when, in reality, Adam Smith preached Laissez-Faire, a hand's off approach so that the Invisible Hand can tell us what direction to take. The Invisible Hand is Consumer demand, the Stock Market, the Commodities Market, Economic Indicators and the sound of that still, small voice inside of you that tells you go shop.

So, I met with my Marketing Guru and, as we sat and talked, he turned to the financial institution crisis that was going on at the time and said to me, "All this is solvable. The problem with any economy is the people. In Europe, it's the tradition that gets in the way of the governance. Yes, natural disasters have changed civilization and disrupted life for the people of the earth, but it has also acted as a motivator, pushing us always to greener pastures, new technologies and higher ground. As a result of the financial crises, we find ourselves in an economy that needs to create jobs that generate income.

To do this, we must understand that jobs in factories are less efficient in today's world with the costs of oil hovering around $100. It's sure not $12 anymore, like it was in the 20th century. What do we do? We create enterprise for the 21st Century. We invest in the individual, in entrepreneurial education and we teach the Magic of Marketing. Why drive to workplaces when we can work over the Internet? So, with the voice of a Cantor, smooth and calm and melodic, he went on to say….

Chapter 2-Marketing: The Entrepreneur, the Forest, and the Tools

A lumberjack, working his goods
Climbed up a steep hill and there stood
He stopped to relax
And, leaned on his axe
While seeing the trees from the woods

What is this thing we call marketing? We can't touch it, feel it, or hang it on the wall, can we? So, what is it? One answer is that marketing is the movement of products, goods or services from the producer of the same to consumers of the same. The reason we can't touch, feel, see, hear, or sense marketing is because it is a process. The marketing process is age-old. From trading between tribes, to world-wide shipping under sails, to hawkers and vendors that traveled from village to settlements to towns, marketing has been with us throughout history.

Like anything else in this world, marketing, in both concept and practice, has changed. No longer do we trade fish from villages by the sea for meat from villages in the forest, we have supermarkets that provide us with the means or process of consuming what is produced. It's a complicated world we live in, and the marketing systems are just as advanced. We need to know about the system if we are to be successful in any marketing efforts.

We also need faith to be successful. Faith in ourselves, in our ideas, and in the system where we will move our product, goods, or services to the consumer is the key ingredient. Faith is based on a thorough understanding of the structure of the marketing system, how it works, and how to make it work for us. Faith makes giants of small companies. It is the bedrock of our belief is our idea, our belief that there is an actual need out there that we can meet. Our faith is the basis for our business philosophy, our goals, and our plan. If we have enough faith, and enough knowledge of the marketplace, and the way in which the marketplace works, we will succeed.

With our faith solid and intact, we can begin our journey to the heights of success. We can reach the mountaintop, the pinnacle of achievement in our field, be it business, charity, or government, by understanding that we must know what's going on around us. We must be able to see the forest from the tress, so to speak, and be able to categorize that information, effectively. As an entrepreneur, we must journey to the top of our "resources" or "assets" and look over the opportunities that are available to us from that point of view. To do this, we must know the way to the top, and the equipment required for making the journey.

For the entrepreneur, the journey to the mountaintop will be hazardous and slippery if we have no direction. Our direction, like the stars as indicators to a navigator, is our "philosophy", our reason for being in business. "Progress is our most important product", so says General Electric. "Honda, we make it simple", says Honda. Progress and simplicity, not appliances and cars, are the reasons these companies are in business. Oh, they make money, no doubt, and lots of it. Yet, the reasons for their entry into business, the "need" they saw in the marketplace, was their philosophical "Way" of doing business.

The entrepreneur needs to understand what it is to be taken on this journey to the mountaintop. Our idea, or product, or service must be concrete in our minds before we can set our direction or philosophy. If we bake cookies, are we providing a tasty snack, or a convenience (where you buy it), or a necessity (as with diet cookies). If we write computer programs, are we providing a product (the program on disk), a service (fixing other programs on disk), or an idea (how to fix other programs on disk) .If we are trying to solve transportation needs, we will need to carry along more accessories than we will if we are trying to meet snack food desires. If we are pushing a political perspective, we will need more means of persuasion than we would for selling bread or flour. If we are selling jet aircraft, we would need more technicians, engineers and test results than we would need if we were trying to sell blue jeans. All we take is our product, our "resources", and we seek to find the opportunity that will allow us to make a profitable exchange.

What we take determines how long we must travel, what obstacles and challenges we will encounter, adventures we will survive, and ...most importantly, how we will pack our bags, or become <u>organized</u> for the trip. So, you see, it is the process of organizing around our idea, given a philosophy of how to meet consumer needs, that is the first act of our journey. We will become organized to a greater and greater degree as we approach the mountaintop, and we will be even more effective after we have discovered the difference between the forest (the vague, complex marketplace} and the trees (the opportunities for us).

The entrepreneur must have a definition of marketing that meets the need for effective philosophy creation, goal setting, and planning. Marketing is a discipline that springs from the field of Economics. Of course, the definition of Economics is merely the allocation of scarce resources among alternative uses, according to Adam Smith, "the father of economics", in The Wealth of Nations. We see, therefore, that marketing can be defined as a process of distribution or trade between producers and consumers in an effort to allocate scarce "resources" among alternative uses, or "opportunities". But, what about the entrepreneur?

An entrepreneurial definition of marketing might be: "the design of organizations to effective channel resources toward a goal of securing opportunities within a specified sector of the marketplace in an effort to find a position which maximizes resource utilization". In other words, the most important consideration in an entrepreneur's definition of marketing is the point of view or philosophy of the organization toward the market. That philosophy, translated into an appropriate organizational structure and process, will allow the entrepreneur to position his venture in a place in the market that is void of competition and returns maximum benefits, based on the resources at his disposal. We call this a "niche".

It's like gambling at a casino, you play at the table where you have the cash to survive. That's your best position. You sell the product that you best understand to the people you best understand. And, you get the information you need, that perspective or point of view of the market you are entering, to plan and manage your marketing program. That's your best position. And, you should organize to take maximum advantage of it.

Chapter 3- The 4 P's: the Tools of Marketing

Mixing stuff can bring great joy
Like Cakes and stews, or Christmas toys
But, when the mix is not thought out
The outcome is in doubt

To start, everyone in marketing should be familiar with the idea of the marketing mix. The idea, here, is that there are four ways of thinking about managing the marketing function of a business, the marketing function being the practice of selling based on a logical evaluation of the best way to sell. The marketing mix concept is the idea that we can think about marketing, that intangible set of skills, in the sense of manipulating product, price, promotion and placement...the 4 P's.

We find that the marketing tools, the 4 P's, can be mixed in such a way as to carry out the function of marketing. The order and priority that we give to the 4 P's is dependent upon our market. If our product is new, promotion may be effective.

If the market is full of competition, pricing patterns may be the key. In either case, placement of the product on the supermarket shelf... or in the movie houses, or at the car dealership, or into a vending machine, is very important. We make marketing mix decisions based on what we can afford, what we are selling, and to whom we are selling it. This requires information.

So we start with our product, our idea for something we believe people will buy. We believe they will buy it because they are just waiting for the right deal. They may buy it already, but we can sell it to them cheaper. Or maybe they would buy it as soon as they discover it solves their problem. We know they will buy it. How do we know? We have faith.

To price our product, we need a little more than faith. We need to know our cost. We also need to test the waters of our faith, or the level of demand for our product, at least to determine the degree to which people will pay no more. As long as all the bills are paid as a result of sales over a yearly period, each year, the price is right even if we sell only one item. But then we have the responsibility to charge the most the customer will pay. Its good business to do so since there'll be times when the customers will have their way. And, sometimes they will not believe it's good if it isn't expensive. That's marketing for you.

Then there's placement. Placement means putting the product in the hands of the buyer. The wholesaler, the government contractor, the housewife, the retail outlet, or the T.V. viewers, all are buyers. Our job in the placement process, formerly referred to as distribution, is to find out where people routinely look for what it is we sell. Beer drinkers go to bars, book lovers go to book stores, music lovers go to record stores, and voters watch the news. Whether it's the placement of a car in the showroom, a dress in the store window, or an ad in the daily paper, placement is the legal act of contracting with the people who use or resell your product. The idea is in putting it where it can be retrieved.

Finally, the last of the 4-P's is promotion. Promotion is the act of telling people about your product, its virtues and utility, its price and accessibility, in a way that grabs their attention and educates them to the point of a sale. Education is what promotion is all about. Through public relations events, through advertisements, the foot-in-the-door salesman, or a bright and shining package, the promotional effort is designed to get the customer through the door to buy. "If you build a better mouse trap the world will beat a path to your door", is an old saying. But to be on the safe side, you'd better tell them where the path begins.

Marketing management is the function of managing the marketing mix, juggling the "tools" of product, price, placement and promotion within the framework 'of a budget. It is the act of organizing, staffing, directing, coordinating and evaluating the entire marketing program to maximize profits. Planning sales territories, hiring salespersons, setting sales quotas, providing promotional materials and training, and overseeing periodic sales meetings is an example of the act of marketing management. Keeping in touch with the finance people, new product R&D folks, and the advertising department is another. Manipulating the 4 P's to keep the organization in business is the job of the marketing manager. Remember, no sales, no salary.

Chapter 4-Know Your World: Marketing Intelligence And Market Research

Sherlock Holmes of Scotland Yard and every private eye,
Have the knack for finding fact and circumventing lie.
Just like research scientists, while looking at the sky
The way to find the answer lay in how you cut the pie.

Have you ever gone fishing or hunting? Yes? No?

Well, if you've gone fishing, you understand the process of marketing intelligence. No, this is not going to turn into a spy novel, it's a fishing story without a lie. You see, marketing intelligence is just like fishing, you can't see beneath the surface but you know the fish are there. Similarly, you don't know, in business, what kind of world you face, but you do know that it's full of currents and full of sharks. A quarter of the American population changes residence every year. There goes your list!

The economy fluctuates in different ways at different times. New laws come in, old laws are superseded. Your competition wants your clientele. The act of allocating organizational resources for ascertaining general information about the environment is marketing intelligence. Whether it's socializing with a Congressman at the country club or hobnobbing with competitors at a national trade show, it's that public relations function that keeps you abreast of changing times. It can be the perusal of the newspaper, or library research, or direct mail questionnaires to potential clients, the idea is to know your world in order to know your industry and the relative impact of trends and changes on your company. You don't know what will become a problem, or what will be an opportunity to make money, but you want to know beforehand. So you fish.

A good way to keep track of all this "intelligence", or useful information about your world, is to categorize all your collections into six areas. Most businesses believe that data of this general nature can be classified as pertaining to demographic, economic, social or cultural, political or legal, technological, or the strengths and capabilities of competition. Census data and other relevant statistics of population trends, as they affect your business or distribution networks, are examples of demographic information.

Similarly, a word from the elderly lady across the street that the landlord intends to go condominium is information about a future change in the service area's age and income makeup. Economic trends can affect any business. Buying patterns change, if the prices of substitute products decline. A factory layoff, caused by energy price changes in the far reaches of the world can affect the ability of a business to maintain supply levels.

Social and cultural considerations can be explained by stating the obvious. The French buy crêpes, Americans buy hamburgers, housewives do the shopping, and the affluent class travels by jet. As far as political or legal actions that affect a business are concerned, local zoning laws, legislation to determine drinking age, labeling requirements on cigarettes and other products; and the regulation of industries by state and national agencies are examples. Technology may impact your industry and your business if your competitors adopt a new method of making a product cheaper. Wouldn't it be better if you found out first? And then there are the sharks, or the competition that is present and lurking in the wings of other industries. Keep an eye on them.

So now we know that there is a lot going on out there that we need to be aware of and understand. We need to know everything we can about our world, about our industry, about our product, about ourselves. But, most importantly, we need to know what we don't know. We fish to find the catch, the information that tells us if we need more. What is happening out there that will indicate, through trends or significant events, the fact that we need more information in order to make a decision. A decision that will allow us to gain the advantage and prosper.

This organized and categorized data helps us make a sound decision that will keep us afloat. A decision that is supported by facts. We fish for signs and signals, ah yes ...but now it's time to hunt.

Market research is the act of hunting. It is the search for a particular piece of information that we are missing to make our decision an effective one. Marketing intelligence keeps us aware of the trends and changes in the environment, but market research tells us how to take advantage of them. It's a hunt for missing information.

The motivation of buyers, the impact of environmental changes on our prices and line of goods, the need to relocate product placement, or the requirement to change our advertising slogan are examples of the kind of answers we are hunting. Some practitioners in the marketing field believe that our comprehension of the marketing forces and factors in the environment gives structure to our philosophy or direction through the wonderland of the marketplace. From this, hypotheses of the best methods to maximize clientele are formulated. Market research is the process of hunting for those answers by asking the people who need what we have.- At least those we think need it. Ask any way you can, but make sure the answers are the markets, not your own.

The process of market research is similar to a hunt. Instead of fishing for a bite, a signal, a sign of activity, a forewarning of change, we proceed to track down our prey. That prey is a "fact" that we gather by following tracks. We follow the tracks that are laid by our search for an answer to our hypothesis, our hunch, our faith that there is a reality in the marketplace, yet unrevealed. We state our hypothesis and we start to follow the trail. The public library is a great place for research already performed.

The government may have information on the subject. If all efforts to find the answer through previous efforts of others does not present a definite answer to our specifically-stated market research question, like <u>who</u> will buy, <u>when</u> will they buy, or how much will <u>they</u> pay for it, we must go directly to the marketplace for the answer.

We ask our customers, our potential customers, our competitor's customers, and anyone that has a potential need for our product. We ask on the phone, we ask through the mail, we ask in person, we ask others to ask. We want to make sure we don't shoot the cow instead of the deer. We use statistics and other techniques to hold our expectations and biases in check. We want the buyer's answers ...the deer. And, as an old proverb states quite clearly..."don't sell the skin of the deer until you have shot it". We want to ask the right people and get the right answers.

Chapter 5-The Customers

Caveat emptor, buyer beware
Paid too much money, don't despair
Should have left it on the rack
Just wear it once and take it back

Now that we know we have to ask to get answers, the question becomes: Who do we select and why? Well, that's a good question! We have to ask everyone, in a sense. We have to ask everyone because, in some cases, we have something to sell but we don't know who really needs it. Or, there are situations where we are sure of who needs it, but we don't know if they are the only ones. So we ask everybody until we find those folks that need it the most or will pay the most for it. Remember, we have faith in our idea and we're looking for the kind of people that can have the same faith. Their faith will be based on the fact that our idea is a solution to a problem in their lives. In other words, they need it.

Why would they need it, this idea of ours, this product? They need it because it either saves them from thinking, or moving, or working, or it removes obstacles to their thinking moving or working. They like time-saving devices, telephone bill paying, medicines that relieve headaches so they can get a new headache learning to use the new computer that eliminates the obstacle of calculation. They buy flowers because the shop is near the office, lunch for the same reason, and secretarial services, just because they don't have to move from their immediate area. Products, other than necessities, that save energy, activity, or effort, sell in America.

People buy three types of products: the things they need, the things they think they need, and the things they like to have. All of this depends upon the income, education and social standing of the individual. To some degree we all fall into these categories in the marketplace. People are responsive to products in two ways: they buy out of habit or they buy as a response to a crisis. To simplify our concept, we can say that people buy necessities out of habit. They buy the same items from the same stores at the same time of the month. We can also say that people buy what they think they need if they believe a crisis situation can be averted with the product. Fire and smoke alarms, icing for snow days, flowers for anniversaries, and aspirin before the cold season, "better get the oil filter checked".

And, finally, people buy what they like to have because people like to have it. Why do they like to have it? Ask them: More than likely it's a matter of habit, or without it their life is in "crisis".

There's something we need to remember about the buying public, the customer, the consumer, or our client. What we need to remember is that they are basically creatures of habit. They drive to work using the same route every morning. They eat in restaurants that are the most familiar. They buy toys for Christmas gifts and flowers for anniversaries, as the season dictates. They live in patterns and practices that are reinforced and supported by other members of their groups.

Their peers all dress the same" look the same, admire the same, live in the same style, and generally earn the same, talk the same, and come from the same background. Practitioners in the field of marketing call these groups of consumers or buyers segments of the marketplace. It goes back to what we said earlier about the French buying crêpes and Americans buying hamburgers. A segment of the market that buys a particular product is a group of people with common characteristics. Whether they need it, or think they need it, or just like the idea of having it, the kinds of people that buy a product are generally cut from the same cloth. It's something we need to remember and, as effective entrepreneur types, to note for future reference. So, just like the deer we were hunting, once you've seen (or recognized) one of them, you've seen them all. And, if it's true what is said that "where there's smoke there's fire", it likewise should follow "where there's deer, there's bucks ".

To organize, without disguise, the way we sell our wares
Is predicated, most of all, on which group really cares
By seizing opportunities, our resources expand
And, we get rich, and find our niche, by following the plan

Let's go back to the organization and its design.

Remember, we must put our resource house in order, to be

effective. We must design a comfortable fit between our

product, its process or production, and that part of the

organization that determines the amount of product we

should make. This is called the marketing function.

Of course we have to be concerned about finances.

But, finances are dependent upon how much we sell. We

need to attract good people, the best people, and they

should be recruited depending upon our needs in

production, or administration, or sales.

Everything we do, every step we take, every role we

create, every communication channel we establish, every

procedure and policy we institute should be based on our

projection of sales.

Sales projections, or a plan of revenues for the organization based upon anticipated demand for our product, can be developed in one of two ways. The practitioners in the field of marketing use either the breakdown method or the buildup method of projecting sales. A good entrepreneur will develop sales projections, for each fiscal period, to be used to measure sales performance in terms of established quotas for salespeople, and to provide his banker with a justification for loan requests and subsequent repayments.

Using the breakdown method, the market researcher will analyze the industry and its growth potential, factoring in economic, political, demographic, social, and technological influences that can change or impact that growth. Interest rate changes, new legal requirements, technological innovations that may attract customers to other industries are examples. An attempt to quantify these factors is required in this analysis, in terms of the dollars that can be expected for the entire industry for the coming year. This analysis can be limited to industries, localities, or expected trade in a shopping district, but it must include an analysis of your company's share of the pie.

Once you have determined the impact of all external forces in the market environment on your industry or sector of that industry, you want to ascertain the impact of competition on your business. You need to see who's fighting over the pie.

This analysis gives you your expected share of the market. For example, if the industry generated $20 million in sales last year, and the economy is expanding at a rate of 10% over the coming year, this indicates an industry sales level of $22 million for the coming period. We should expect our share to rise by the same increment. However, if our competition has increased its promotion and advertising, we may not get our proportional share of the 10% if we are not able to advertise at the same level. By breaking down the activity from the environmental level, to the industry level, to our own level, we are able to develop a sales forecast that is justifiable and meaningful.

The buildup method is just the reverse. We ask our own sales people, customers and experts for their educated opinions about future orders, sales potential and anticipated demand. By gathering data from all sectors of our organization and clientele, we are able to put together a picture of future sales potential for each territory, each product in our line, each region of our market, and each customer classification. Putting it all together gives us a sales projection that is, again, justifiable and meaningful. Different industries or product orientations will require different methods of projecting sales.

Use what's best for you. But keep records. You'll find that a banker is impressed with lofty sales projections, but is more impressed with 40,000 letters from potential clients saying "yes" to your inquiry about their willingness to buy your idea. If such letters are the basis for your projections, you'll have no problem with the banker about the loan, since he'll have no problem demonstrating his confidence in you.

Sales projections are important in terms of the entrepreneur's planning and subsequent management of the selling season. You have something concrete to use in your evaluation of results and you are provided with realistic expectations. Everything should go well if the sales forecast is well done. But things do change and unexpected situations arise. It is the nature of life, the nature of business, the nature of the non-profit environment, "the way it goes", so to speak. We must be ready for change, for surprise, for obstacles, upheavals and adventures. These changes are the kinds of things that turn entrepreneurs into conservative businesspeople and conservative businesspeople into frustration.

Entrepreneurs can gain ground by breaking ground when change occurs in the marketplace. They seize opportunities and capitalize on turbulent activity. They introduce new products, compete with established institutions that are not organized to address change, and transfer technology to areas where that technology shakes existing market structures and buying habits. Look at MCI, Apple Computers and Turner Broadcasting to see what I mean.

But, conservative businesspeople don't like change. They don't like competition or obstacles to their sales projections, or new ways that require changes in old ways of doing business. They become frustrated by change until they realize that the organization is the only thing that must change to survive. Marketing intelligence systems that were designed to alert the organization of changes that could affect it may be outmoded. The right questions may not be asked in the current period to effectively alert decision makers to outside forces in the environment. Complacency, due to long periods of success leads many to believe that nothing will ever change. A good fisherman knows that even the currents under the sea change over time.

Marketing intelligence systems have changed with the introduction of computers. Everything must change. It's up to the organization to change, to meet changes in the environment that cause changes in the marketplace, before the change is necessary. New forces require new methods.

To put it all together, an effective organization should be designed to find a market segment, keep it, add to it, and adjust to any threats to it over time. You get an idea and you want to put it into action. You want to go to the wonderland known as the marketplace. You've got to get there and find your place in the sun, your position, your image. And, you want to be seen in that position, in that light, in your advertising and placement. You want to be seen as NUMBER TWO, if you're Avis in the car rental market. You want to be seen as people who "earn it", money that is, "the old fashion way", if you're Smith Barney in the securities market. YOU want to be seen as the people who let you "have it your way", if you're Burger King in the fast food market. And, in terms of placement, you'll make sure that there are Avis Rental facilities at Airports, Smith Barney Securities dealers in financial districts, and Burger King Restaurants near schools, factories, and well traveled roads.

Promotion and placement are the most productive tools we can use to position our product. As long as we can cover our cost, the cost of the product, the people making and selling the product, and all of those "necessities" we need to be in business, we can price to the maximum amount that people are willing to pay. Sometimes we charge more for one item than we do for another, but that's because, sometimes, people buy more of one item and less of another. But as long as we make a profit on the whole operation, all of our sales, we are pricing effectively and maintaining our position.

Once we've found our position in the wonderland of the marketplace, a position where the sunshine of prosperity and a stable clientele warms our pocketbook and our self esteem, our faith pays off. If it should rain, from time to time, through changes in the economic or social climate, if the waters beneath our boat become choppy as a result of competition or changes in the law of the land, we merely reorganize our people, processes or policies in order to stay afloat. We may even throw out old products for new ideas. Remember, it's the clientele that brings the money. If they want new products, and we can provide them without jeopardizing our position, let them get those goods from us. It's our position, our image of service, our posture of meeting needs, their needs that we want to protect. We will stay in business, fishing for trends of change, hunting for answers to consumer problems, and selling to the public through an organization designed to find a position in the

marketplace that maximizes the utilization of our resources.

Chapter 7-The Details of Placement

The farmer went to market just to sell his lot of grain,
And, when he saw the marketplace, he had a great disdain
He hadn't really thought of it as sunshine turned to rain,
But, soon he realized that people can be very vain.
No one appeared on this bleak day to buy his lot of grain.
No one came to purchase in the middle of the rain.
The marketplace was open-aired, unsheltered, in the main.
Not the place for selling in the middle of the rain.
No one wanted clothes, or face, with spots or mud or stain.
So, no one came.

What does a marketing practitioner mean by

placement? Is it the concept of distribution, the movement

of the product after processing, manufacturing, harvesting,

or assembly, to a wholesaler or retailer? Is it the process of

packaging, storing, shipping, warehousing and displaying?

It seems that placement is the concept of distribution. That

is, physical distribution between organizations and brokers,

between producers, wholesalers, middlemen and the retailer

to the hands of the ultimate customer. It is the exchange

relationship between a manufacturer and the multitude of

outlets, both direct and indirect, that bring the product to

the buyers. It is the display, or presentation of the product

on the shelf, rack, counter or wall of a store, shop, or

gallery that is the natural, most reasonable <u>place</u> to find that product. A product which meets the buyer's particular need or satisfies a particular want. Placement includes all aspects of distribution, with the primary goal of locating the product so as to make it <u>easiest</u> for the buyer to buy. Placement is the ultimate goal of product distribution.

So, let's look at it from the perspective of the buyer. Where would you look for something that solves your problem or satisfies your specific need at a point in time? Let's not forget time and situation before we answer that question. Times change, society changes, people change, and likewise, distribution systems change as well. Supermarkets replaced corner grocery stores , suburban shopping centers replaced downtown shopping districts, and shopping through cable television and the Internet will replace driving from shop to shop. In addition, situations change from time to time. People are willing to travel to New York or Paris for a designer dress, paying above market prices and travel expenses, to add to their collection. The same people will purchase a set of horsey at the local convenience store if there is a social affair to attend in an hour, and, their stocking have developed a tear. If you have to have it, you have to get it where you can, and you look where you believe it can be found. Time and situation determine the place a shopper will look.

In terms of the product, marketing practitioners have determined that shoppers buy based on the degree of prior consideration given to the purchase. The more expensive and durable the product, the greater the degree of consideration, or thought will be made prior to the purchase. The less expensive and less durable the product, such as "necessities", the less consideration the buyer will give. Automobiles and diamonds require a lot of prior thought on the buyer's part and are considered specialty goods. Groceries and beverages require little prior thought and are called convenience goods. Some products are so special to buyers, they will only purchase them from establishments they can trust and rely upon. They trust them for their reputation of quality and service, the way they "treat" customers. Products in this category, the higher end of specialty goods, are called shopping goods because the place where they are purchased is more important than the product itself in satisfying buyer needs. Thus, image is everything.

So, here is the question, again. Where would you look for something that solves your problem or satisfies your specific need at a point in time? You'd look in the place where that something, that product, is most likely to be found. Thank God for the mass marketing system. As a buyer, you would look for automobiles at car dealerships, beer at bars, diamonds at jewelers, videos at video stores, or record shops, or street vendor stands, (have we reintroduced competition).You look for dresses at Lord & Taylor, Zayre's, Sears, the Gap, Mimi's Boutique or on the rack of a street vendor, depending upon whether you were looking for a <u>convenience dress</u>, a <u>specialty dress</u> or a <u>shopping dress</u>.

You would look for milk at the supermarket, a dairy food processor, a farm, or the local convenience store, depending upon how much milk you wanted and where you are physically placed (have we reintroduced demographics). You buy that milk at one of these places depending upon your situation, whether it's lunch near a construction site or preparation to feed the Cub Scout Troop (have we reintroduced buyer motivation). You buy it based on your need and its intensity, your habits, and the availability of the product placement choices based on competition in the marketplace.

Now, let's look at placement from the standpoint of the entrepreneur. The question that arises from the entrepreneur is this: where should we place our product, given what we know about our segment of potential buyers (people with common characteristics and demographic distribution who potentially will buy our product) to make it easy for them to come and get it? The answer is this: we find out where they are, whether they are in one spot or scattered throughout the country, and we contract with outlets that traditionally move our type of good. If our choices of traditional outlets (wholesalers, retailers, etc.) are limited or unfavorable in terms of cost or other contract arrangements, we open our own outlets. If our potential clientele is distributed unevenly, or is scattered across the country, we establish a mail order service or create a telephone marketing and shipping distribution system. We call or they call, and we ship it out in the most timely or least expensive way. And, if they are concentrated in one city, or several specific locations, we send out salespeople with product, or promotional material, in hand. From the standpoint of the entrepreneur, we want to find out the most efficient, convenient and cost-effective way to put the product in the hand of the potential buyer.

Psychologically, (and let's face it, 90% of it is psychological) we want to determine the patterns of people and place our product, accordingly. We want to support and reinforce traditional, established buying habits for products, goods and services in our society because it makes distribution relationships easier to develop and maintain. We want to be sure that potential buyers will come to our stores, shops or vending stands because...that's where they always come. We want to be sure that they always go to the shopping center because...that's where they always go. We want to make sure they continue to buy gas at gasoline stations, so we can sell them cigarettes (watch the no smoking sign). We want them to shop at Wal-Mart for back-to-school clothes, so we can sell them lawn equipment. And we want them to buy groceries at the supermarket, so we can depend on a source of customers for T.V. Guide, People Magazine, and The Enquirer.

We are conservative business people, we entrepreneurs. We want to be able to depend on long-term customer behavior so we can make long-term contractual relationships with our distributors. Long-term agreements mean stable prices, stable shipping cost, stable production schedules, stable employee levels, and stable profits. It is better to know you have money coming in than to worry about finding buyers. Conservative businesspeople come from satisfied entrepreneurs.

But, what if consumers change? As we said, everything changes. Customers move, competition arises, rents increase. What happens to the conservative and satisfied businesspeople? They become entrepreneurs, of course. They wake up (if they ever went to sleep) and start fishing and hunting, again. They keep an eye on customer trends, customer habits and changes in demographics, buying patterns, and competition.

They beat the competition to the <u>placement</u> punch by providing drive-in banking, photo-processing and fast food service. They build outlets in new housing developments, put vending stands near new office complexes, and pick-up and deliver for everything from typing services to automobile repair. They find any way they can to provide an opportunity for their segment of the market to get its hands on the product before the other guy does it. They promote their location to make every member of that segment acutely aware of where the product can be found.

America's dynamic public is constantly moving around and changing its mind, and can forget your name, your location, and your product. New entrants to your service area may not be aware that you exist. If you open a new location or sell through new distributors, people need to know where you are.

Promotion serves the clientele, the potential customer, and the possible customer, as well. It sure serves the entrepreneur. Let people know where they can get that

great stuff you've got on the market. Because people move,

you should move. And that movement, in the marketplace

and the business, keeps the entrepreneurial spirit alive.

P.T. Barnum had a circus, once upon a time.
Mr. Barnum made a statement, but it had no rhyme.
"A sucker's born most every minute", he said these words so
true.
But, if he didn't have his circus, he'd be a sucker, too!

Promotion, what is it? Funk & Wagnall's New

Standard Dictionary says of the word promote, the base

word of promotion, "to cause to move forward to some

desired end: contribute to development, establishment,

increase or influence of, faster; further; forward; encourage;

advance; as, to promote a business enterprise. Funk &

Wagnall are right on the money with that definition, 'cause

that's just what we want to do with our 'business

enterprise...or our non-profit, as the case may be. We want

to cause our business organization "to move forward to

some desired end. That end being the goal, in terms of our

mission...our direction. We want to contribute to the

development, establishment and increase of our enterprise,

our organization, by fostering and encouraging awareness

and knowledge of our product, good, service or organization. We should be fostering customer development, influencing people to buy from us, and encouraging our clientele to be loyal repeat customers through advertising and public relations.

Flip Wilson, a prominent American Comedian of the 1970's would often say, "What you see is what you get." That's not necessarily so, however. What you think you see, if it's what you think you need, will get you close enough to come and take a look. If it's what you think you want, if it really solves your problem or satisfies your desires, you'll buy it. Promotion is the idea of getting people to try your product by letting them know that it's there.

Now, how do we go about the business of promoting our business or our organization, and letting people know what we've got? Before we answer the question, let's go back to a concept we need to consider first. Let's go back to the concept of targeting a segment of the market.

As you recall, a segment of the market consist of people who have the same needs, desires and goals. These people, as opposed to other segments with different needs or goals, buy the same kinds of products. Now, let's remember, people can be part of more than one segment, buying products from more than one producer. However, the entrepreneur is only concerned about the segment for his product and few others.

Let's explain further. There's a concept among marketing practitioners known as product differentiation and marketing segmentation, two concepts that are understood together. The idea of product differentiation merely suggests that different segments of the market (market segmentation) will buy the same products at different prices or with different product qualities. It's like having a fire drill at a large university. Only the people in the building near the alarm will respond. Those who never hear the alarm, because they're in a basement or in a sound studio, will not respond. If we want to sell smoke detectors to students at that university, we probably would be more successful with the students who always hear the alarms. They'd probably be aware of the possibility of fires and would more than likely have a psychological need to feel protected. Conversely, the other students who never hear the alarm may not be as acutely aware of the possibility of fires. Their demand for smoke alarms would probably not be as great. So, we'd probably have to lower our prices to sell to students who were "unaware" of the fire alarms, or we may be able to raise our prices in selling to the "very aware" group.

If our research indicated that the "very aware" group lived on the top floors (as a demographic), were people who are early risers (sociological), and/or were people who had been exposed to fire experiences before (psychological), that segment would pay more than the others. Or, if we modified our product to add a music alarm or an accessory that automatically warns of chemical fumes in basements of closed places, we may be able to increase sales among the "unaware" due to their ability to utilize it for their particular needs. It's like selling baking soda to use as a deodorant for refrigerators and garbage disposals. Although the product was designed for culinary purposes, people in a different segment (or need) will buy it as a solution to their problem. Sometimes you don't even have to change or modify the product, you just have to convince the marketplace that it can be used, as is, to solve their problems. And, that's where promotion comes into play.

People need the necessities of life...food, clothing and shelter, but, most of their buying decisions are based on beliefs about what they need. The brand name of the food, the store it comes from, the price, the convenience, the service, the ambiance, all are promoted to assist buyers in their decisions. The quality of the product, its utility, durability, and contribution to one's status is usually promoted. So is price, which is very important, and the availability in terms of placement. We've got to let them know where it is, and how conveniently we're located. We have to let them know to help them decide, on us! And, don't forget, our competitors are selling, too.

So, what is promotion, I mean, really! It is the process or activity of creating attention, awareness, and understanding, through the act of educating a segment of the market, on its own level, about a product, good, service, or organization. This is done through the utilization of management tools know as the "promotion-mix". The promotion-mix, just like the marketing-mix, can be manipulated, prioritized and juggled to achieve the goal and consists of 1) advertising, 2) sales promotion, 3) personal selling, 4) packaging, and 5) public relations activity.

Advertising is the act of creating a message specifically for a segment of the market, organizing that message into an orderly, easy-to-read statement (called copy) which can be understood by the selected segment, and presenting the message through a medium (TV, radio, magazines,...you know) that the segment most likely receives. It's like placement. College girls watch soap operas (they have the time), beer drinkers watch football (or vice-versa), teenagers listen to radios, the middle-class reads the news...stuff like that. The key consideration, and not to be forgotten, is to create commercials (or flyers, brochures, business cards, letterheads...stuff like that) which catches the attention of the buyers in that specific market segment. Do your hunting, your research. Find out to what they respond and to what they don't respond. You can't make buyers aware of your product, its placements, its prices and its ability to solve their problems, and allow them to solve yours, if you can't get their <u>attention</u>.

The difference between advertising and public relations is basically direction and money. Advertising is the purchase of media services for the business in order to achieve the goal of increasing sales. You want to check with the medium (TV, radio, magazines, etc.) to see who looks, listens or reads. Do they reach your people, your segment, and your clientele? They have this information available so they can sell you and others advertising. If they reach the people you are trying to reach, make yourself an advertising budget to reach everybody you can (or almost everybody) and spend the money on the most cost-effective (people per dollar) mediums, first. But, don't forget to experiment and change priorities from time to time. Consumers do. And, don't forget to be "creative". People respond to advertisements just like they respond to products, those that meet their needs get their attention.

Public Relations consist of activities that are not geared toward a direct increase in sales, but are designed toward a general increase in sales over the long haul. Public Relations is the practice of making people feel good about doing business with the organization by reinforcing positive images. This helps the organization fulfill its mission by gathering support. The more support, the more customers that will be recommended, the more recognizable the commercials, and the easier it is to contract with distributors.

The most support, the greater the reputation, the more likely market intelligence will be easy to obtain, and the less likely the community will allow your organization to fail. If folks like you, they'll support you. If you give to the United Way, the March of Dimes, or the local Ballet and Symphony organization, (unless you are the local Ballet and Symphony organization, which means you give free concerts to underprivileged children), they'll support you and you'll survive. Besides, it's good publicity. It's good for your image.

Publicity is free. It's the favors you earn with media people which gives them incentives to publicize your sales promotions, and you. A sales promotion is anything you can do to get positive publicity, or to generate a lot of customers at one time. Holiday specials, guest appearances by celebrities in your store, free gifts to the first inflow of customers, rallies, joint-promotions with complementary products and distributors, and any other "good ideas" are examples. When a baseball team has a BAT DAY, or provides free tickets to underprivileged children, or donates proceeds to charity, this is a sales promotion and it attracts media attention and positive publicity. You may even lose money on the event (God forbid), but you'll gain a lot of new customers who feel good about doing business with your organization.

Sales Promotions, whether they are public functions

or options for customers presented by sales staff, bring benefits for customers for a long time to come. People begin to expect it from you and look forward to being involved. It preserves your image. If you want to see a good example of what sales promotion is all about, go to your local bar on St. Patrick's Day.

Finally, as a noted commentator on public affairs once said: "the medium is the message". He is right, too. Television, radio, newspapers, magazines, billboards, posters or word-of-mouth can transmit advertising or publicity. Each medium, by its very nature, has a different impact on the general public and specific segments of the population. Choose your medium wisely. Send messages about your product or organization through channels of communications that will have the most favorable impact on potential buyers. Send messages through several channels to make sure it gets to your market segment, but be sure to coordinate the promotion campaign so that the message you want gets through. Remember, media, like business, are people. Find them, get to know them, work with them, be creative with them, and give them the faith you have in your goals and direction. And, remember, as the saying goes, "It pays to advertise".

Chapter 9-Creating Markets

You can solve the people's yearning
If you dare, if you care, and you have the time to spare
By assisting them in learning
If you swear to be fair and you think in air that's rare

It was Sunday, March 17th, St. Patrick Day, 1985. I was watching the NCAA college basketball play-offs on CBS television. It was exciting, interesting, and ...my team won. It was the thing to do if you're a sports fan on a Sunday in March. But, like all good things, it ended. And after the games, what else do you watch but Sixty Minutes. The guest for the first segment was Fidel Castro, President of Cuba.

Now, let's understand that this is St. Patrick's Day, 1985. One week before, Premiere Andropov of the Soviet Union passed away and was replaced by Gorbachev at the top of the Soviet Union. All of this occurring right in the middle of strategic arms negotiations between the U.S. and Russia. Castro did not attend the funeral. Instead, he appeared on Sixty Minutes, one of the most popular programs on American network television. He had an idea he wanted to sell. HE knows how to do it. What else, but television.

If you turn on the TV, you'll notice that more and more commercials are designed to sell ideas. If you can convince people that, through the most powerful of media-television, the idea you support is a valid one, they will support it. You get their attention, first, and then you compete with other advertisers to educate them to you side. Whether it's the support of Cancer research, the political ideas of a presidential candidate, or the idea that "a mind is a terrible thing to waste", the ideas are translated into dollars for foundations, campaign chest or the United Negro College fund. You've got to get to the people, the segment that has a need for a tax-break or to feel that their own ideas are being promoted, to get your idea on the public agenda. To do this, you've got to create a demand for it.

Creating markets for ideas, innovations or existing products is a legitimate goal of an organization that has defined its mission and direction. You must have that faith we talked about, but sometimes to be successful, you must create your own demand. How do we do this? We use our imagination, the media, and our fishing and hunting skills to find unfulfilled needs, underutilized distribution channels, and untapped markets.

People need everything! If God made it, and man can modify it, it can be sold. There are thousands of products on the market that, many would say, are not needed by the people who buy them. Yet, they do buy because they believe they need them. For status, for entertainment, for leisure, for work, or for religious reasons, they buy.

As an entrepreneur, it's easy to see how this presents an opportunity for creation of a new market. Every day, inventions and creations from computers to computer software, from labor-saving devices to cook-books of the latest sex-symbol are patented or copy written in the United States. Annually, in recent years, over 600,000 patent applications are filed with the U.S. patent Office and 500,000 pieces of copy written material are submitted to the Library of Congress. It starts with an idea, an idea of a new way of doing something. An idea you create for a process, or a machine, or a modification of a machine.

Everybody has ideas about improvements in their workplace. I'm sure everyone, at one time or another, has heard a co-worker or outside observer say something like, "why don't they try to... or "haven't they thought of", in response to an observation of a problem. People make money from ideas. Suggestions by company employees, in many corporations, result in bonuses and cash awards. Sometimes, more often than not, these suggestions require no capital investment. They're just changes in the way things are done. If a simple idea about a process can pay dividends, cash dividends, to an employee at a plant, think what a thoroughly researched and sufficiently financed idea can mean to an entrepreneur. A little risk-taking, a little sweat-equity, a little cooperation with suppliers and distributors, and you're looking at a million dollar company.

Engineers get paid to think up ideas. Bankers get paid to evaluate market potential and probable financial success. Why not get paid, as an entrepreneur, to take the risk of commercialization. Commercialization is the act of taking an idea about something and turning it into a product that is a success in the marketplace.

The idea can be almost anything. It can be a process, or a product, or just an idea that other people will support-like tax relief. A man in California, Howard Jarvis, started what became known as the tax payer's revolt, a freeze on property taxes, and sold the idea to the people. He started the idea of reducing state taxes and raised enough money to promote the issue of a referendum ballot on television. In June of 1978, Proposition 13 was passed by referendum. This measure reduced property tax rates on homes, businesses, and farms by 57% in California. This vote limited tax rates to not more than 1% of the market value and valuations to a growth limitation of not more than 2%, unless the property was sold. Panic set in among those who believed deficits would prevail, but the idea was a successful sell due to the development of grassroots support.

The ideas of nuclear freeze, anti-abortion, women's rights, contributions to the United Nations, drug abuse, telecommunications reform, and teenage pregnancy have all been formalized through organizations and promoted to raise contributions of cash. Anything that can find a constituency, a segment in the market, people who like it, need it and will buy it, can be commercialized.

The <u>commercialization process</u> involved six steps, as I see it. They are 1) general research, 2) specific research, 3) innovation, 4) testing, 5) selective marketing, and 6) general marketing. Whether it's an idea, such as the formation of an association for small business people or a product, such as a new recipe that will provide people with a pastry of high quality and limited calories or a process such as a method of speed reading and total retention, it can be developed, packaged and promoted. We first want to perform general research, designed to determine what the market needs and what will satisfy that need. This is similar to the process of marketing intelligence, or fishing, we talked of before. It's also similar to laboratory research conducted by scientist at major corporations. You just fiddle around until you come up with something that has potential for "commercial value". In our case, as entrepreneurs, we just want to see what's happening out there that indicates a possible opportunity of an unmet need, an underutilized distribution system, or an untapped segment of the market.

We may find if we are ex-football players, enterprising financiers, or the owner of a cable television channel, that there is a need for more football to fill the hours of our cable channel and provide a source of revenues from increased advertising. We, like ESPN, Donald Trump (former owner of the New Jersey Generals), and others, may start the United States Football League. We may decide, in time, that the need is still there and form a relationship with NBC television and the World Wrestling Federation to create the XFL Football League (also defunct). If that doesn't last (and it didn't), we might decide to find some women college basketball players and create the Women's National Basketball Association. Hey, how 'bout Arena Football!?

We might get together, if we have the mind to, and create all new channels, such as the Women's Channel, the

History Channel, Black Entertainment Television, Fox News Channel, Oprah TV or MSNBC (Bill Gates and NBC together), all of which were started in the 1990's. ESPN also began operations around this time and has expanded into "sports bars", as well. But, although our general research may indicate a need or desire for football all year round (USFL, European Leagues and all that), although we have access to underutilized cable channels and stadiums, and although we can find fans in markets where there is no pro team, we need to conduct specific research which is what the USFL and XFL did. That's true for the Indoor Soccer or Lacrosse Leagues.

Specific Research, like marketing research, targets particular issues and concerns that need to be addressed before an innovation can be created or proclaimed. Demographic, sociological and psychological questioning and re-questioning is performed until a complete picture is developed of a specific need that must be addressed. This is often done through Focus Groups.

People will say, "Sure" to a question about whether they would like something to be available, but when you start to quote prices, things can change. Where would be the best place to locate? Are the people really in support of the idea? Can they pay, will they pay, and will enough of them pay? What colors do they like? Specifics! Specific when, where, what, how and how much are the questions. It's like that scientist in the corporate research department. He thinks he has something, but he has to run it through some analysis to be sure. Voila! Innovation!

A new idea, something that is unique and practical for the marketplace. A jump ahead of the competition. A new process or a completely new product. A new way of serving the public. An idea that fills the void. Like the USFL or XFL that once provided Spring professional football for home entertainment and family outings. Now we have indoor football or arena football all over the country. Like the WNBA that provided basketball during the summer months, and highlighted the physical accomplishments of women, capturing markets as a result of their unity in competition (and television rights). And, there's cable television itself, in the distribution of TV programming.

Remember, in 1980, there were no rock videos, no Internet, no DVD, and no cell phones. No toothpaste in a pump dispenser to eliminate waste. No replaceable plastic nails in case one breaks (or doesn't), to name some product innovations meeting market needs. And don't forget the Olympics every two years as customer drawing activities or examples of creating distribution.

There's satellite television to capture the untapped markets in rural areas, and trade with the world through the Americanization-franchise opportunities. Sales of Coca-Cola in China, McDonald's in Paris and Wendy's in Beirut,

Lebanon. The mailing of free samples of new products, from cereals to perfumes to Internet access software (let 'em try it, they might like it). Innovation, to paraphrase the dictionary definition, is to introduce something new, or as if it is new. Innovations capture the market for entrepreneurs that have faith in their ideas and its ability to meet an unanswered need. An innovation in distribution, be it the fast-food restaurant, financial services at the insurance company or bank, or the creation of Disney World in Europe, redirects the buying patterns in the marketplace because it anticipates a desire for change before it happens. Innovation revolutionizes companies and organizations that foresee a crisis in a forgotten or neglected market segment, by promoting a product where there is not competition and a big head start.

Before any innovation can be successful, it must be tested. The USFL started with a few teams before it expanded. Disney Productions started out with Disney

Land before creating Disney World, and Euro Disney. Now, everybody's got a theme park in their backyard. Just like the scientist in the laboratory, a product, process, or idea has to be tested to see if it works. If it's a product we're talking about, it must be tested in a laboratory, and under some conditions, must meet government specifications. If it's a process or idea, the test comes in the marketplace. And, as with a new breakfast cereal or dress design, if it flies, take it to the general public.

The process of commercialization of an idea takes time. The steps can be easily defined in some instances, while in others they all mesh together. As the entrepreneur, it's your job to take risk. If you believe in your idea, the process if commercialization will be a joy and challenge as you create new markets and a new future for us all. Have fun and don't forget the media, the greatest creator of new markets in our society, our world.

And, speaking of the power of media in promoting ideas, let's return to Sixty Minutes program of St. Patrick's Day, 1985. After watching the show and sitting through the three segments that dealt with issues from race relations, to the cost of hospital care, to Fidel's ideas about American foreign policy, the program turned to its segment on letters from viewers. The last comment made by the viewers was a letter regarding a program, a week before, on the pollution of a California wildlife Refuge by contaminated water, piped in to irrigate nearby farms. There was a letter from the federal government, stating that they intended to close the Wildlife Refuge mentioned in the story, and would proceed to shut off the water that polluted the Refuge. This water, although contaminated, did help farmers in the area to irrigate their crops. The issue between Environmentalists and farmers was heated, as the story was presented, but the government did act.

Why did they act? The power of media! The power of Sixty Minutes! By putting the issue before the public, a consensus was created, an idea was sold. By getting the story on sixty Minutes, support in the public domain, in the marketplace of ideas was created. Action on ideas, innovations or existing products comes from creating an image in the midst of the public, the marketplace. Media, for ideas, innovations or existing products, is the ox that moves the cart of new market structures. Create a market, position yourself and make a profit through selective media management and your faith.

A buck or two will help us through
The passage of the trial
A dollar here, a penny there
Can turn a frown to smile
The tribulation of this life
Is sometimes hard to bear
But, through it all, you never fall
If money's there to spare

When one talks about creating new markets, you can't help thinking of the quantum development of the communications industry, in America, since World War II. I mean, before World War II radio was the mass medium and each major market city had two or three major newspapers. Today, radio is secondary to television, even though radio has shown a rebound in listeners, stations, and revenues. And now we have satellite, digital radio everywhere. Although most large cities only have one major newspaper, several smaller tabloid publications for specific segments have arisen. And, there's a city magazine for each "big town". The Washingtonian, the Atlantian, Houston magazine, Memphis Magazine and others are examples. There's also a couple of national newspapers around to show you how times changed. But, the bigger winner, from cable, to direct broadcast satellite, to low-powered stations, to the increases in independent outlets, is television.

Why the rapid development in the communications industry (also reflected by so many Communications colleges opening at major universities since 1965)? The answer lies in improvements in technology, increased demand for information, and the need in the economy for added sources of advertising distribution. America became the undisputed economic champion of the world, following World War II, by directing its wartime manufacturing capability toward consumer satisfaction. Information and education about product utility and availability became the key to achieving production goals and ultimate consumer satisfaction.

The medium of television opened doors to mass

markets, and mass markets opened doors to TV. We can watch a series of commercials an easily determine a) the target population, b) why they are trying to reach them, c) what their product is, d) how they make creative decisions, e) when they select advertising times, f) where they choose to advertise (media mix selection), and g) how advertising/promotion strategy is created and coordinated.

Where do we start? As I was told by an experienced television producer, "Your market is where there is a need, not where you want a need to be".

As this relationship expanded over the past few decades, the "vast wasteland" of television has become an advertising research laboratory. By observing commercials on TV, one gets an idea of a company's target market, its demographics, socio-cultural composition, and psychological makeup. A lot of marketing intelligence and research goes into determining where your market exists. It's a match of resources and opportunities. You have a product, goods, or service, you want to sell it to people who are willing and able to buy, that need or desire what you have. It solves their problem. But, they must know that is solves their problem and how it does so. When advertising, you want to present all aspects of marketing mix, the 4-P's, to your potential buyers.

You want to tell them, a) what it is and how the consumer can use it, b) what is the cost and what arrangements or considerations are given, c) where it can be found or how one can get their hands on it, and, d) the availability of promotional information that will educate them further about its use, cost, and availability. But, before we start, we've got to know who has the need and where they are.

You might say that the process of creating advertising involves six steps:

1. Determining the psychological motivation that indicates a need for a product;

2. Defining social and cultural characteristics of people which indicate a high probability of motivation for the product;

3. Selecting demographic (geographic, age, income, etc.) areas where there is a high probability of motivation for the product;

4. Creating the message, with psychological, social, cultural and demographic symbols and images which will motivate buyers to seek the product at the appropriate place;

5. Selecting media to send the message that traditionally, or by design, is a source of information for the market segment defined above; and

6. Creating a plan to advertise and measure its effectiveness in terms of dollars spent, sales developed, and attitudes toward the message.

All this is done in the context of matching

opportunities and resources. The opportunities are the motivations of people to meet specific needs. The resources are the products, goods, services, or ideas that meet those specific needs. Marketing intelligence, the fishing trip, and market research, the hunting expedition, are tools used to ascertain the <u>motivation</u> of the public for your wares.

Everybody that has the need may not be in the same social class, or the same income level, or the same ethnic group, or even the same location. But, they will have one thing in common: A psychological motivation for a solution to a consumer problem that is the same. Your product brings them together. It's a market segment. Talk to them.

To determine the psychological motivation of the buyer is easy. There are two things to do. One is performed by the entrepreneur and is purely mental. The other is performed by the marketplace and is mostly physical. First, the entrepreneur merely needs to look at the product and turn his or her thoughts in the opposite direction from creativity. He or she must look at the product utility. What can this be used for, and by whom? Baby shampoo is being used to deodorize garbage disposals. Throw-away shaving razors are being used by women. Mineral oil and iodine is being used as tanning lotion. Home economists are always finding new uses for old products in household chores. Old clothes can be worn in new ways. New technologies can be applied to old problems. There are hundreds of uses for a skill, talent, process or product. There are many benefits to the implementation of an idea. The entrepreneur, like the research scientist at a major corporation or the chefs in General Foods' kitchens, must find new ways and methods of using the product. As you do, make a list.

The marketplace, in order to determine needs and motivations must be surveyed. Psychological questioning, be it by mail, phone or interview, should be designed to determine the basis for buying. Why do they buy a product? What is the problem they seek to solve or avoid? Is it fear that makes them buy burglar alarms? Is it the pride that makes them wear designer clothes? Or, do they wear designer clothes for acceptance, or quality or fit? Is it comfort or self-esteem? Are people angry about politician's policies? Do they fear his policies? Do they like his smiles? Do they like some things because of a sense of vicarious accomplishment?

I'm sure you know of people who see themselves as being a part of a great movement, while they don't like others because it conflicts with their beliefs? A good survey, periodically given and adjusted to social changes, can give a lot of information and save a lot of resources down the road.

This survey process should include a look at what kinds of people have the same beliefs, the same attitudes, and whether there is a strong relationship between the psychological need for a product and social status or cultural background. It could be that upper-income people, having more money to spend are the most frequent travelers to Italy. The social factor of being an American will cause most people to buy souvenirs while visiting Washington, DC or Mount Vernon, or Gettysburg or Williamsburg. What Irishman doesn't wear green (anything green) on Saint Patrick's Day?

And, where are these people with this psychological need? Are they in rural areas where cable TV reaches housewives and farmers? Are they Baptist that watch the Christian Broadcasting Network (CBN) and love all religious artifacts, or weekend athletes that always turn on ESPN (the sports network) for the latest game or event? We need to know where they are, who they are, and what they are looking for to meet a need in their social life or place in the culture. We need to know why they need it, that product that solves the problem. We need to know the motivation. If we know this, we can find the market for our product, we can determine how to effectively reach these people, and we can determine how much it's going to cost to get out there in the competition for the minds and hearts of those buyers.

Once we've determined our segment, all those motivated buyers spread from the valley to the next mountaintop, from every income level, social class and cultural background available, having in common the same motivation...the same need, we can develop our copy. Copy is a practitioner's term for the message we want to send to the buyers to motivate them to buy from us. They're motivated to meet their needs. We want to direct that motivation to our doorstep. Our organization should be uniquely designed to provide relief in their search. We have to tell them, now that we know who and where they are, that we can satisfy that need.

By using symbols and images which are recognizable to them, because of culture, ethnicity, geographic residence, or their state of being, we can attract their attention and begin our education process toward the purchase. We want them to see a symbol and remember our company. We want them to see an image and remember they had a headache... yesterday. We want them to relate to our organization because we have a celebrity spokesperson that's from their part of the world. We want them to give us their attention because we talk as they do, look as they do and understand their needs. That's our image, and we'll give them a brand symbol to remember us by when they go to the store. Charlton Heston means the NRA and Joe Camel means cigarettes.

When putting together copy, or our message to the buyer, our advertisement, we always keep in mind the relationship between the motivation of the buyer, the requirements of the medium, and the relationship of the symbols and images to the needs of the buyer. We want to make sure that everything, I mean everything, is directed toward stimulating an interest based on the buyer's motivation. We want to get the buyer's attention for without it the advertisement will not do its job. We want to design the advertisement, its message, so as to begin the process of educating the buyer about our product...its attributes, its quality and uses.

Different buyers, having different needs, will seek solutions through different media and different distribution points. There's market segmentation and product differentiation, again. One product, several uses, several ads, different media, all designed to reach different markets. Thus, different copy, but...the same image of our product, and, the same brand symbol to remember us by at the store.

However, if there is a different use in different segments of the market, we must relate our images and symbols of the need, the problem, and the motivation present in the buyer to our copy. It's like using children to sell toothpaste to grownups and using grownups to sell toothpaste to children.

When selecting media, keep in mind the motivation, the problem of the buyer, and where they would look to solve it. People looking for jobs look in the classified ads of a newspaper, but people looking for entertainment look in the movie section. Doctors read trade journals when selecting medication, but people with sunburn rely on TV commercials and ads in newspaper travel sections. Sometimes people buy auto parts upon the advice of their mechanic. Other times they buy on the advice of a clerk at an auto parts store.

How did the buyer get to the store, or the auto dealer, or the local mechanic? He got there through a TV ad, or a sign in the window, or through word-of-mouth. When you ask people to tell you about the problem, their need in the marketplace, don't forget to ask them where they look for information to solve that need. Put your ad there and try to design it to get their attention, educate them, and motivate them to buy. In order to make it all happen, you need a <u>plan</u>.

Once you've found the market, gathered the information on their habits, and created a way of getting through to them about your products and ideas, you need a plan. The attention- getting process of advertising doesn't happen overnight. People are busy with their lives, their families, their careers and just getting through the day at work. There are competitors out there, ravenous "sharks" who are selfish about their portions of the market. They'll advertise, too! Not as well as you will, nor will their product be as good, of course. Nevertheless, they are there. So, it takes a lot of time, creativity, and perseverance to get attention in the marketplace.

You've got to know how much it's going to cost to create an advertisement. Psychologists, sociologist, artists, media specialist cost money. There's a need to sustain your presentation, your message to the segment, over a period of time to allow it to be noticed. Your ad may be great, it may grab the audience and generate cheers, but it still takes time for everybody to read the newspaper or catch it on TV. So, you develop a schedule with media people to determine the best times to catch your folks, the right time of year to use print, the right time of day to buy radio time, or the number of pages to send in junk mail.

You cost it all out. You decide on priorities. What's the best way? What's the next? What medium complements another? What medium do your buyers "believe" the most? Do you need to change the message according to the medium? Can people really appreciate an automobile if it's not moving in a newspaper or not seen on radio?

Do paintings sell at all, sight unseen? After you've talked with media marketing reps and perused the library reference section for "rate-data" information on print and broadcast media, put it all down on paper. And, for certain products, goods, services, and ideas, don't forget word-of-mouth. It's the most effective, most direct, most reliable, and most trusted advertising ("A satisfied customer is our best advertisement"). Start a publicity campaign of your own.

Advertising is a great thing! It allows the entrepreneur to take an idea to the public without leaving his craft. It brings the customer to the door, over and over, while you stay at the plant and produce.

It is to the American free enterprise system, the grease that smoothes the wheel. It gives the opportunity to the hobbyist to write a computer program and sell it by mail through ads in a computer magazine. It gives the small town promoter the opportunity to open a night club and attract clientele from all over the country.

You can start a magazine, sell your own design of dresses, provide tax services to the housing development, or raise money for a child's transplant operation.

Advertising, well researched, creatively developed, and properly distributed, can make any entrepreneur's dreams come true, and reward him of her for their faith in earthly goods.

Chapter 11-Technology: The Endless Growth Economic Model

It seems that every time we talk, the phone sounds far and thin
It seems that fiber optics haven't reached our local den
The idea that we can be reached by Internet is strange
Technology is passing me, can that be rearranged?

Malthus was wrong, of course, or we wouldn't be here. For those who are not familiar with Reverend Thomas Robert Malthus (1766-1834), noted classical Economist of the 19th century, the complete title of his essay is entitled, "An Essay on the Principle of Population as it affects the Future Improvement of Society with Remarks on the Speculation of Mr. Godwin Condorcet and other Writers". His work was a response to Condorcet's writing, "Political Justice", which was anonymously published five years after.

Malthus, it seems, had a theory that was very current for its time. He preached in England in the 1800 's and spoke and wrote a theory of Economics that suggested that food production increases arithmetically, one field, one planting and one yield, each year, in an arithmetic ratio based on the yield per acre of field. He also postulated that people increased geometrically. That is, one man and one woman equal one, two, three, or four or more children, each in turn producing geometrically from generation to generation. You know, two and two are four, four and four are eight, eight and eight are sixteen, sixteen and sixteen are thirty-two. That's geometric. So, Malthus figured that one day, war , death, pestilence, and disease will catch up with us all, starting with starvation because people will increase geometrically while food production will increase arithmetically, leaving us scrambling for crumbs and roots. Well, what Reverend Malthus left out of his theory, and what sustains us to this day, improving the yield per acre, is technology. Malthus didn't considered technology.

What is technology? Webster's dictionary describes technology as: "The application of scientific knowledge to serve man in industry, commerce, medicine and other fields" It's a procedure or method of performing an activity or process. It is the means by which a function or action is improved. It's a way of doing something.

Technology has been adding to the productivity of industry, commerce, medicine, and other fields from the beginning of known history, and even before. The carving of a bone by primitive man for a sharp hunting instrument is an example. New techniques and furnaces for melting iron and copper, forging them together, created stronger swords and permitted the Bronze Age warriors to conquer the Iron Age warriors is another. When the Arabs designed a sail, it made it possible for ships to sail into the wind and move commerce more effectively. The discovery of penicillin helped cure many infections which previously killed thousands and brought about a longer life span.

But technology is something more, at its roots. It is humankind's way of using ingenuity, imagination, inspiration, and reason to create a new idea and proceed to build that mental image into an archetype, then into a functional product, good, or service, and from there into a mass market concept that can serve the interests of as many people as possible. Technology, therefore, is our way of solving practical problems and improving productivity. Because each time a new technology is introduced, it solves the problem by making the work easier, quicker, faster, or a lower cost.

What is the endless growth economic model, you ask? I believe that the economy, unlike the doomsday preaching of Malthus, is ever expanding and ever growing. If you look at it, there are always more, better, and less costly products, goods and services in the economy, particularly when you consider the growth from the primitive economy through to the mass-market economy in which we live today. A writer named W.W. Rostow wrote about this some time back in the 1950's. He postulated that, in terms of economic development in the world there are five stages of growth. These five stages are: primitive society, preparation for take-off, take-off, the industrial society and the mass-market economy. The idea is that, from the beginning, economies have grown from a primitive stage where people farm, gather, hunt and trade among other people near them. Without airlines and railroads, what else can they do? From that stage, economies enter a preparation for take-off stage where infrastructure and economies of scale are created. In this stage, technology is introduced at a level that coincides with roads and river travel and enhanced communications. Think of India in the 1950'in comparison to India in 2012 as an example of the difference between a primitive society and a preparation for takeoff economy.

From there we reach the take-off stage or the stage where the Russian Empire became the Soviet Union. In that case, the Soviet Union created industries through periodic economic plans that had stated goals. Obviously the economic structure of the Soviet system was not the best way to go, but it did serve to bring 19th century Russia into the industrial age. In the take-off stage, think of the United States at its economic peak following World War II. Then, the country had a strong infrastructure and a powerful industrial base. So, everything hummed along in the 1950's, and then...we entered the mass-market economy where consumer consumption and mass-market distribution took hold. That's today' economy.

So we have moved into this mass-market economy where technology is increasing productivity and consumption at the consumer level through the various stages we've traveled through over the last fifty years. We had the nuclear age, the computer age, and the information age. We had an economy led by railroads, then steel, then automobiles, then computers, then the information technology. Over the next few decades we can envision the increasing power of technological change as we enter an age of telecommunications and information technology infusion.

The role of technology in the economy is the contribution of applied science to the improvement of products, goods, services, or ideas (software, process, training, copyrights, etc). The U.S. Small Business Administration promotes technology through the Small Business Innovation Research (SBIR) & the Small Business Technology Transfer (STTR) programs, the federal government's foremost technology efforts. Through a competitive proposal process, winning firms are awarded contracts to develop a technology product for one of ten participating federal agencies. At the same time, the firms are encouraged to develop the product for the private commercial market.

The Small Business Innovation Research (SBIR) is a three-phased federal government sponsored technology initiative designed to increase small high-technology firms' participation in the government's billion-dollar research and development program. The Small Business Technology Transfer (STTR) program is part of this initiative.

Three Phases of SBIR: Phase I - firms are awarded up to $100,000 dollars for a six-month period to produce a feasibility study to evaluate the scientific and technical merit of their proposal. Phase II - firms are awarded up to $750,000 dollars for a period of two years to begin the actual research and development of Phase I. Phase III - firms are expected to attract private sector funding or non-SBIR federal funding to take the product to the marketplace. To qualify, a business must be a US small business with no more than 500 employees at the time of the award, a for-profit company, and American-owned and independently operated.

The Marketing of technology is a unique endeavor, being strongly linked to its applications and market segments, and the extent of those applications in the society or industry. The technological innovation, the application, is that process that increases productivity. Whatever it may be, how it is applied, who buys it and uses it, determines how to approach the market. The 4-P's play out in the same manner with any other product, good or service.

Technology is an idea that is ready to be used or consumed. If you sell software, find the segment of the market that buys it, promote to them, and price things accordingly. With technology, things are a little different when it comes to pricing because the price has to cover development cost. If it's a new process for making steel (core ten steel), a new use of information technology in selling books (Amazon.com), a new pharmaceutical innovation (a vaccine), or the use of interactive DVD's in education (and don't forget distance learning), it's a market segment that can easily be identified. Know them, wow them, and price for immediate sale so you can raise the pricing once they are "addicted."

The extent of the application in the society or industry simply means that the market segments may be many. Software used for accounting has been sold for household use by simply taking out the complicated routines. A new idea can be applied to a government contract, developing something that can also be sold to the general public. Our society uses many inventions that came from the development of technology to fight World War II. You can use video and digital technology for making assessments about your golf swing or your dance moves or your acting skills, providing automatic feedback. And, you can use lasers for eye surgery as well for a cutting tool in fabricated steel production.

Technology and innovation, new ideas and new methods, all bring an increase in productivity to the economy. The marketing effort should sell to those segments that use and need technology applicable to the solution to their problems, be it industry, commerce, medicine or other fields. The fact that what is being introduced is brand new has implications that are different from consumer goods. Development costs and the uniqueness of utility play important roles in decisions and organizations around technology.

We always need more and better products, processes and improvements in technology. The economy grows by the injection of productivity. Prices always rise over time. That's economic growth. Yet, the average price for an innovation declines as production increases due to the movement of the organization from a limited technology segment to the general consumer market. TV, VCR's and computers are just a few examples. Not long ago, the number of VCR's in households was around 3%.By the end of the 1900's, it's around 89% of all U.S. households. Now, people have DVD's. The same patterns occurred for radios, TV sets, computers, microwaves ovens, and fax machines. The economy is always moving forward and growing with the advent of technology and the increase in population. That's a fact.

Thinking people must also be creative salespeople in this endeavor. The same principles apply as with the sale of any product, good or service. The more you know about the market, the more you know about the buyers, and the more they know about you, the better it will go. Have a good trip!

Chapter 12-Marketing Strategy: Putting Together a Plan

Once upon a time there was but nothing in the pot
The people were quite hungry and they argued quite a lot
The Piper brought a rock to them and showed each how to build
A fire and a crock of food, their bellies they did fill
With grill, and krill, and will

Now, once we've worked our way through the forest, we've found our food and we know our way to the top, we have to put it on paper. A marketing strategy is a vision, a philosophy, a mission, and a goal. We still must have faith in ourselves and our ideas. Then, we know we can get to the top because we have visualized it. We know, for example, that we have to do something to get them to respond. We have to have a vision of the need that we can see, unmet and unchallenged. We know we need resources and we need to search for opportunities. We know we need to build an organization that is geared to dealing with the problem. No, we don't need fifty-five players, no not eleven players, this is NOT football. We need the right mix.

The Strategic Marketing Plan is derived from the Marketing Strategy. What is a marketing strategy? A marketing strategy is that road map, that path you decide to follow that will bring you in contact with the largest possibility of finding deer, if you're on a hunt. It's the knowledge of where the fish bite and what bait works when fishing. It's your vision from the top of the hill.

At this point, we need a new level of perspective. Thus, a strategy is a vision of the opportunity to meet a need in the marketplace through an action approach that follows a philosophy that serves the organization. Is that too much?

In short terms, your strategy is the planned actions you will take over time to develop a market that you believe in. Your strategy is the long view. What do we want the world to be in five years, twenty years or more? Your strategy envisions tools you may not have now. Your plan consists of the action steps you will take to get there.

I'm reminded of a small restaurant that I frequented a few years ago. It was located in Washington, DC just two blocks from the White House, near the World Bank Group complex and adjacent to the downtown DC business district with all its high-powered lawyers, lobbyists, financiers and think tank institutions. This place had an outdoor café under a canapé and a beautifully designed and comfortable interior. They always catered to a very upscale and worldly customer base. Artwork decorated the walls as part of the restaurant concept.

The owners were beautiful people and had spent their lives building this business. Times changed and clients departed due to the urbanization process and office shuffle. They wanted to retire but they didn't know how to make this business work again. The events of September 11th, 2002 accentuated conditions. The problem was the shortfall from after lunch (normal dead time) and after work, "happy-hour" crowds.

The only other promotion they ever had was a sponsorship of a local softball team in the young professional league around the White House. The restaurant volunteered a case of beer for the team before each game and the team wore the restaurant logo on their uniforms. After the games, the team would come over and drink three times the cost of the case of beer, and made it known among the young professionals that this place was one of theirs. Business grew.

The wife-partner owner was named Sarah. She and I would sit and talk when I came by. She always stopped to sit with long-standing customers. She was part hostess and part manager, and she was well liked too. These people were from Argentina and had grandchildren they wanted to see.

So, one day I made a suggestion. She didn't like it, the suggestion that is; because of reasons I couldn't understand. As time went by, I made other recommendations only to find that she would find a reason it would not work for her.

Finally I had a conversation with her about some other family matter and she mentioned something that made me understand her, and her position. She had built this business on a high-end market, which was supported by the client base that since moved or relocated entire offices. Some of these local businesses downsized over the previous few years. Many forces were impacting on this enterprise and she was not willing to take chances with her investment. This is understandable.

A few weeks later, inspired by some kind acts by this beautiful restaurateur, I decided to sit down and help her decide what her strategy should be. Not her wishes or her longing for the past, but her strategy for moving this asset.

The idea was this. I was watching television the night before. It was pledge week on the local PBS station.

On this evening, the program was a visual tour of Italy called, VISIONS OF ITALY, its land and its monuments, from a helicopter point of view in digital, high definition television. It was spectacular and I endorse it.

I suggested to the owner that she use this tape series for an afternoon, after lunch coffee time. Play the video on all the TV's and serve a top quality coffee (Jamaica Blue Mountain), and call it TEA TIME: Out of the office in the afternoon and around the world. Make it upscale, relaxing and international...a place to be found at Tea Time. And let them sit outside and smoke cigars from 2PM to 5PM (sounds like a joint venture with the tobacco shop, to me!!!) and offer a coffee drink from day to day.

Sell it as a mid-day coffee hour for executives, secretaries, and other power moguls, and sell that tape. Make coffee combinations with pastries or sandwiches. Sell the coffee at low margin, but price it for the concept.

Since the PBS affiliate showed the tape to help

raise funds during its pledge week, I suggested that she call

them and create a formal representation to raise money for

the station. She was given tapes and a display. She

promoted the tape and sold eighteen in two weeks at a $250

pledge level with the tapes as premiums. Later, people from

the PBS station would stop by for lunch or drinks after

work. A crowd began to form, again. This was a new

crowd. The energy, and those who first caught the feeling,

brought more of the same ilk. With this short act, things

changed, but they changed because she developed a

strategy.

TEA TIME evolved into a semi-monthly "talk" in

which prominent businesspeople and scholars from local

universities would sit and talk and listen to lectures on the

events around the world. Women began to attend with more

frequency as time went by and the DC smoking ban was

introduced into law. This intensified to a point where it

became a formal series of power lunch lectures by

prominent Washington political and foreign affairs dignitaries. Broadcasters soon joined the process. When the smoking ban came along, we had our people and we easily worked around that.

I asked her, "Why are you in business?" she gave me the normal story, family, children, retirement and all that. I said no to her answers and prodded her into the real reason she wanted this business to succeed. Her final answer was, "I like to serve the best food to the best people, and I like for them to appreciate it". And thus began her strategy because she knew and stated her purpose...her mission or philosophy about doing business. From this point on, we were able to sit down and write out these and other ideas. I encouraged her to bring her husband into the discussion. Top management should all be involved and should support the effort. Together we set down and wrote up a short, one-page thing that gave us:

a) a Philosophical Position or Mission-Raison d 'etre,

b) a set of goals and objectives (sales, customers, etc.),

c) a Campaign Theme that connects us to our people to the common goals

d) a schedule of actions and activities to reach specific goals (i.e., ads, calls, visits, etc.)

e) a budget with anticipated returns

f) an organization and delegation of responsibility and coordination,

g) a set of agreements with participating parties (coffee seller, fund raiser recipient, etc.)

So, let's break that down. After the first two-week "test period", things went well. We agreed that, if things didn't go well, if we didn't get the response we wanted in customer counts or a significant rise in the percentage of gross profits for that time period, we would stop and cut our losses, knowing we tried. We also knew that, since we were committed to a "mission", we wanted to make sure we attracted the level of clientele we wanted also. This was a key goal or we may as well sell pizza. We knew one last thing as well. We knew we were committed to meeting that mission, "serving the best to the best".

We also thought to use that as a theme for our campaign, but thought better of it when we realized that a direct approach sometimes heightens expectations. We wanted this to work because they liked it, and appreciated it. We put out a big colorful sign to announce our "Specials". We printed letters and flyers with a tasteful expression and presentation. We placed ads in weekly publications we knew lawyers and lobbyist read for professional reasons and we set up a web page mailer/announcement for all those who "sign the book" at our encouraging. We made it look like we spent money on the campaign. We did.

The theme was stated continuously: TEA TIME: Out of the office in the afternoon and around the world. We did everything we could to promote this concept to those people we believed had time to sit and drink coffee and meet and do business in a sidewalk café or inside an art deco bar. We hung pictures from well-known and local artists, rotating them (photographs as well) and offering them for sale.

A percentage of the proceeds went to the PBS station for a while. Then, we realized that time creates diversity. We started using the art sales for other charities and events that came to public attention. We were always out front in the charity game from that point on. We even began to rotate the videos and sometimes invite PBS personalities to guest bartend. For this, we have wine specials, and of course, a contemporary DJ. They even began a fundraiser program where local athletes and TV Anchors were invited to "guest bartend" with the proceeds of drink profits going to the host bartender charity. It worked wonders for our reputation and our off-special business. This leads to catering opportunities for fund raising events. Ain't life grand?

The budget was small. Somebody had to be in charge so that person would be first on the budget. I wasn't going to do it, I gave at the office. The owners were busy enough running the place as it was. So, we agreed to hire one of the bartenders to do it. She would take a contract that paid a base for the time slot and a percentage of the revenues generated at a declining rate as revenues rise. A little incentive is a good strategy.

We spent for ads, printing, and phone calls to follow up visits to nearby corporate contact personnel to make a pitch. We are here to serve you the best because you are the best, and here is where we are, and what we are up to. Hey, get your "TEA TIME: Out of the office in the afternoon and around the world, right here!!!"

Chapter 13-The Marketing of Art: The Difficult Made Easy

Selling Pictures, most of all, was not the artist's game
He couldn't paint and sell, as well, and keep the painting
frame
He lost much sleep and did not eat, he had to break the spell
He hired an agent for the job, and now he's selling well

Art! Pictures, paintings, photographs, sculpture, film and music of every kind, that's art. From tribal artifacts to Salvador Dali, that's art. Art is culture. Art is expression. Art is reality remade, its perspective, its form. As Andy Warhol once said, "It's whatever people think is art." Random House dictionary makes it quite clear (if possible). Art is, as it states: the quality, production, or expression, according to aesthetic principles, of what is beautiful, appealing, or of more than ordinary significance. So, have we progressed? I still don't know what Art really is. But, I do know what people think it is. That's progress.

Looking at art from the standpoint of marketing, we must remember that Andy Warhol was right. Art is what people think it is. But why is that? Generally, people are cultural-social beings that usually prefer expressions which reaffirm their cultural-social concepts of beauty and form. Chinese people love the Chinese style of Art. Europeans admire Van Gogh and Rembrandt because they convey massages about Europe's past, and foundation, and the subconscious feelings in all Europeans. Africans appreciate African sculpture because it looks like them and expresses moods and attitudes with which they are familiar. "But what about jazz?" you ask. This is an Afro-American expression of orderly, but syncopated, sound that is appreciated and applauded by Europeans and Asians alike. Well, it's like this. Jazz, like Chinese tapestry, European paintings, and African sculpture, can be appreciated for its expression of beauty by the hands of mankind.

So, let's get on to selling this Art, these paintings, prints, songs, and statutes. The question is: Who buys and why? Before we answer the question, let's remember what we said before. That is, people buy for two reasons: to solve a problem or to prevent one. Is this true of Art? Yes it is. People buy Art to decorate, to impress their friends, to preserve the culture and to appreciate it, or entertain themselves. People solve problems with their purchase of concert tickets. The can eliminate problems by purchasing works of Art for anniversaries and birthdays.

Art lasts longer than flowers or candy and can be displayed more frequently than diamonds. Art allows you to express your status and well-being...your class. Art can give you a tax-deduction and provides a tangible means of preserving your culture. An Art purchase does all this and more. An Art purchases provides one more benefits to the buyer than just solving a problem or preventing one. Like real estate (good real estate, that is), Art is a constantly appreciating investment. So, an Art buyer is, in many ways, an Art investor.

Art is also symbolism, images: Religious, cultural, social, artistic and contemporary symbolism. Art conveys the idea, the perspective through shape, size, color and tone. It's the symbols that people buy. Symbols of peace, beauty, joy, love, pain, sorrow or conflict. There's political art for political people. The work of the old masters (boy, I wish I owned some of that) for old money. There's Pop Art for popular expression. There's subway graffiti for people in touch with the times. All Art has a market. A segment of people that love it, seek it, and will buy it at the right price. Artists should learn to give concessions (two for one deals and such) to sell their wares. A painting sold is a painting sold, and the price of future work rises when it's already out there, so to speak. Artists must find segments of the market that have characteristics indicative of an affinity to the symbolism the artist uses to convey ideas. People who like the symbolism will like the Art. It's like the statement that the medium is the message. If the artist can define the symbolism he or she uses to convey the thoughts, he or she will have no problem finding the symbolism to promote,

134

the symbolism to be displayed by potential buyers, the symbolism of proper placement and presentation, and the symbolism of pricing for that segment.

There's one more concept to be remembered about marketing Art. Art is a <u>shopping good</u>. That is, Art is generally sold based on the name recognition of the Artist or the distribution outlet. Beverly Sills, Izthak Perlman, Stevie Wonder, Ralph Lauren or Picasso have name recognition. The Phillips Gallery, the Kimball Museum, Nieman-Marcus and any outlet positively reviewed by a major publication have name recognition. People with name recognition can give retail outlets name recognition. Look what Jackie Kennedy did for the Peppermint Lounge. Look what everybody did for Studio 54. Look what made Planet Hollywood and Hard Rock Café. Think what a good series of promotional events, coupled with effective publicity (know your media people) can do for you. Everybody knows somebody who knows "Somebody".

Get a name, get a place, and get recognition as a prestigious Art outlet or as an artist with high-class customers. Get promoted! When you have established a reputation as a quality place to do business or an artist that does quality work, you will not only have built a better mouse trap, you will have built the only one.

Sales promotions do promote sales. I knew an artist in Washington, DC, a professor at one of the universities there, who produced paintings for several years, yet was unable to sell them for more than $500 or $600 dollars. He was frustrated with his faculty position and couldn't quite make it solely on Art sales. He had a studio in the artist district, a very spacious place that he used to paint, and think, and worry about his future. As it turns out, he had a brother who was a Jazz musician in New York, as well as an academician at a New York college. His brother worked with a band, in his own studio in New York City, and carried the same frustrations for independence in his Art.

On a whim, my artist friend was asked by his brother if he would be amenable to opening his studio on a Sunday afternoon for a jazz show to allow his brother's band an entre into the Washington market. My friend agreed and they scheduled a Sunday afternoon concert, promoted by word-of-mouth, in early Spring. The concert was a small success, indicating the possibility of greater success with greater promotion. Ironically, as a result of the public exposure to the Art on the walls of the studio, my artist friend sold six pieces of his work that day. As time went by, the two of them "organized" to promote each other's work. The musicians would come to Washington to perform, advertising was used to generate an audience, mailing lists were developed, and paintings were commissioned from the concert crowd. Likewise, my artist friend would take his work to New York for concerts at his brother's studio, lending color and ambiance to what was previously a drab background. More paintings were sold, more people became familiar with the style and quality of the music, and, eventually audio cassettes of jazz performances were sold subsequent to each performance. The "organizing", based on a mission to expose a segment of the market to complementary Art forms which symbolize a specific culture, paid dividends.

Both brothers are satisfied with their organizational image, financial progress, and market support. They have attracted media attention in two major markets and plan to open a concert-exhibition program in Philadelphia in the future. They are conscious of needs and demands of their respective market segments and keep tract of customer characteristics and concerns through casual conversations following each event. They have a plan and, through cooperation, faith, and effort, it's working.

As I write this chapter on the marketing of Art, I am sitting in a college library across the street from the college Art Department, I can see from the window a display of ceramics on the terrace of the adjacent building. There are several pieces of various sizes and colors, various shapes and different designs. I look at these works and wonder, "is this Art?" The answer is that some of it is Art. But, only those pieces that the artist can place in a gallery, or catalogue, or television show, where the people who like it can see it, admire it, and be convinced it meets their expectations of Art, is Art. If that is done, they will buy.

Chapter 14- Social Networking and Getting Started

One for the money, two for the show
Get it all together and go for the dough

This is a new age for enterprise. A new day is here for selling to a broad and deep market, to a shallow and narrow market, to a global market or to the members of your social club, the alumni association or any group, large or small through social networks. We have come a long way from the hawkers in the town square or the roadside food stand. We now have the ability to sell to anyone, anywhere and anytime. This new age phenomenon comes to us through the advent and expansion of the Internet. A whole new world exists that was not even imaginable in the 1950's. This phenomenon wasn't intrinsic to our way of conducting business until far into the 2000's. But, it's here now and it has changed everything.

The advent of social networking, from the creation of the Internet to the social websites and the very opportunity for each and every enterprise to have a globally-accessible identity and capability presentation that is available to the entire market, yours and everyone else's, providing links and connections to related information, and the ability to guide searchers to exactly what you want them to know. It's as if each business, each individual has his or her own global platform that connects to each and every other business or individual. The Internet and the social networking sites have opened the door to new ways to cost-effectively reach markets, make sales, facilitate payments, present sales pitches, provide operating help and promote related products and services, as well as the image and brand of the business. All this, without leaving the comforts of home.

What a wonderful creation. This new age technology and all its affiliated gadgets and connections have made the greatest change to business development since the advent of banking. The Internet, websites, links, connections, list and social platforms (Face book, Linked-In, etc.) provides a contact at very little costs. This is a cost-effective marketing tool that frees all businesses to market effectively. Now, the question becomes, "Who's the target?" That's to say, what goes on the site and how do I get people to come to it so that I can attract them to other related marketing and communications tools such as Facebook or YouTube?

Twitter, Twitter, link connect, this is the new vocabulary of how we meet, reach, teach and trade with each other, here, there and everywhere. You decide. People are inherently self-sustaining and productive, as long as they are free to trade with one another and exercise the creative expression in all of us. This freedom of expression is what each person has that leads to his or her direction in life. Once discovered, it is like the Awakening of the Buddha inside. This perspective provides motivation, from a strategic point of view for the mission through a vision of the possible.

Electronic networks are like any other level of technology in the history of humanity. The technology changes but the rules are the same. A business should advertise where the people who want to buy it are looking for it. You may have to research the multitude of media about how and where to target your base, so you can periodically check to see if they are there, and utilize them as a marketing intelligence source, a focus group for your innovations, a source of referrals for your products, or a customer base on the web. How does this thing work and what should be considered in the design of it all?

The most important aspect of marketing is research, marketing research. You must know the market, the general market, for your product in or out of your industry. You must know your industry, for your products and the other products that are similar in utility or are complimentary. You've got to know your world, the world in which the industry lives, you live. Marketing intelligence...or being informed and up-to-date on your world is paramount for success. Anyone's success.

As an entrepreneur you need to know about competition and new trends, and new attitudes about the product. New ideas of how to solve the problems of your customers that are developed outside your industry could change the demand for your product. You need to know before your competitors know it, even if they know, or because they do know. You must be able to accurately and consistently determine what it is you need to know about the market. Good continuous research means you rarely have to use resources for specific research.

I saw a television program the other day that talked about a newspaper or magazine with a large circulation. They began using the Internet to provide reading content for their brand. As the website began to stream videos, the readership hits declined. People were no longer reading the copy, they were just viewing the videos. They changed

their strategy. They focused their resources on video

productions, almost acting like a mini-all news channel.

They used that platform, that approach, to the market to

target readership audiences, people who like to read or who

have developed a manner of learning from the reading

experience. Older populations grew up reading. They also

grew up on television, but the following generations grew

up without the consciousness of learning without dynamic

visual media. Short attention spans are living with

information competition. The whole world is on satellite

TV or cable or a hand-held electronics with GPS. We have

telecommunication devices with our cell phones and

Internet access. In this world, what you read or watch can

be influenced by Social Media, family and friends, people

who can send readers to a website that serves readers. The

Internet is the cheapest Focus Group available and it can

solicit, screen, gather data, test and analyze any idea

imaginable with just a click of the mouse.

If you look at the market as a fresh baked pie, sitting on a table in a deep dish, with a golden brown crust, you can understand how market research helps to slice it up. Market research helps us watch the hands that reach in to take a piece. The government, the ideas of technology, and social and cultural forces are the ingredients. Demographics, psychological forces, and competition take out pieces for themselves, based on their appetites. Marketing intelligence helps us understand the ingredients and the processes which put the pie together-the baking. There's always eating and baking going on.

If we know the pie, the market, and how it expands and contracts, and moves around in circles, we will know what to do with our pie. We'll have a strategy. We know our mission, why we're eating pie instead of cake or cheese. We'll know our goals, that is, what we can achieve. We'll know our position, where we stand around the table.

Armed with this information, we will be able to more effectively develop products, establish appropriate prices, find convenient placement, and promote what we have to give. We then can organize to do it in the most efficient manner and find our market, our market in a segment of the pie. From our position, we can maintain a direct and determinable access to the pie, knowing where we always are and where the pie is. We have become successful entrepreneurs.

Being an entrepreneur means taking risk, not being stupid. Entrepreneurs are smart. That's why you're reading this book. You really <u>don't</u> want to take risk. You just have to make them succeed. But, you want even those risks to be calculated. Faith in an idea can be turned into a dream fulfilled if we have knowledge of the market. I hope you have it now.

About The Author

Carrington B. Davis was a member of the faculty of Howard University's School of Business and Public Administration from 1973 to 1985. He served as President of the Anacostia Economic Development Corporation, and as the Director of Physical and Economic Development with the Marshall Heights Community Development Organization in Washington, DC. A graduate of Howard University in Economics, he earned a Master of Business Administration from the Wharton School at the University of Pennsylvania. He also holds a Masters degree in Public Administration (MPA), in lieu of a Doctorate, from the University of Southern California. A consultant and writer in Washington, D.C. for many years, Mr. Davis has contributed articles to such publications as The Washington Post, the Wharton Journal, the Atlanta Journal-Constitution and the Baltimore Sun. He is the CEO of Philanthropic Cultural Expressions, Inc. in Washington, DC.

Acknowledgements

I would like to thank the following people for their contributions to the development and refinement of this work, from editing to comments on the approach to the subject. These amazing and talented people include Global Development Businessman, Ponzi Watson, Health Policy Consultant Emerson Hall, Former Deputy Mayor for Economic Development in the District of Columbia, Mr. George Brown, Dr. Prakash Loungani, former University of Tennessee Professor and Consultant with the International Monetary Fund, and Mutsa Karimakwenda, a Washington, DC Energy Policy Attorney.

www.ingramcontent.com/pod-product-compliance
Lightning Source LLC
Chambersburg PA
CBHW051315170526
45166CB00002B/549